MR. WILLOWBY'S CHRISTMAS TREE

Weekly Reader Children's Book Club *Presents*

MR. WILLOWBY'S CHRISTMAS TREE

SPECIAL DELIVERY

NORTHERN TREE CO.

by Robert Barry

McGraw-Hill Book Company, Inc.

NEW YORK TORONTO LONDON

For Puppa

Mr. Willowby's Christmas tree
Came by special delivery.
Full and fresh and glistening green—
The biggest tree he had ever seen.

He dashed downstairs
to open the door—
This was the moment
he'd waited for.

"A magnificent tree! Splendid!" he cried.
"Please, sir, won't you carry it right inside."

"I think it might look best this year
Right in the parlor corner here."

But once the tree stood in its place,
Mr. Willowby made a terrible face.
The tree touched the ceiling, then bent like a bow.
"Oh good heavens," he gasped. "Something must go!"

Baxter, the butler,
   was called on in haste,
To chop off the top,
   though it seemed quite a waste.
"That's great,"
   Mr. Willowby cried with glee;
"Now we can start
   to trim my tree."

When the trimming
   was well under way,
The top was placed
   on a silver tray.
Baxter said,
   "I know just who'd be
Delighted
   with this Christmas tree."

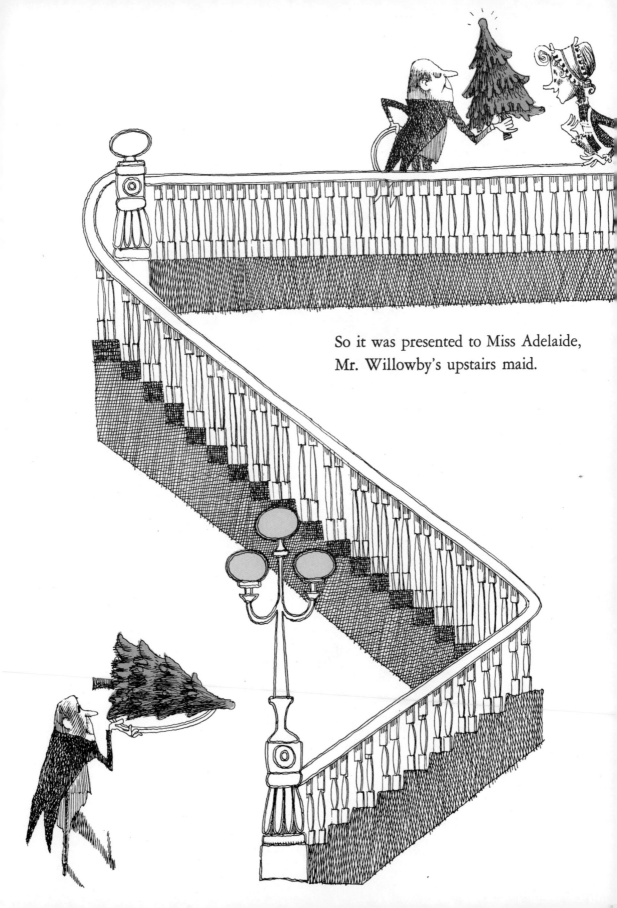

So it was presented to Miss Adelaide,
Mr. Willowby's upstairs maid.

"Won't this tree be a pretty sight
When I have trimmed it later tonight?
But the top, oh dear, I'm so afraid,
Will have to be cut," sighed Miss Adelaide.

And so with scissors
    sharp and long
She snipped off the top
    while she hummed a song.

The top was set out the very next day
In back of the house to be thrown away.

That little treetop caught the eye
Of Tim, the gardener, passing by.
He certainly was not about
To see that little tree thrown out.

He hurried it right home straightaway
To see what Mrs. Tim would say.

"Fa la la . . . Surprise! Surprise!"
His wife could not believe her eyes.

"But our house," she said,
  "is so snug and small
I do not believe we need it all!"

And before Tim had a chance to shout
She cut off the top and threw it out.

Barnaby Bear was padding by—
It almost hit him in the eye.
"Now who would throw a tree away
So very close to Christmas Day?

"I'll take it home, that's what I'll do!
Look, Mama Bear, I've a present for you."

"Isn't it a pretty tree,"
Yawned Mama Bear quite drowsily.
"Before we go to sleep this year
Let's have a Christmas party, dear."

But Little Bear, standing off far,
Cried out, "That tree won't hold a star!"
Barnaby said, "Let's cut a hunk
Off at the bottom, here at the trunk."

But Mama Bear just shook her head,
And sliced the treetop off instead.

"Jolly, by golly!" Barnaby said with a kick.
"Mama, that surely is just the right trick.
Let's trim it with bells and honey rings,
Some berries, and tinsel, and popcorn on strings."

Mama said, "Trim it just as you like,
I've got to tidy up for the night.
This top we won't need any more;
I'll put it just outside the door."

Later on that frosty night,
Frisky Fox came into sight.
He spied the treetop, rubbed his chin,
Opened his sack and stuffed the top in.

He scampered home and jumped his gate—
This Christmas present couldn't wait.

"It's even better than mincemeat pie,"
Said Mrs. Fox with a happy sigh.

Then the Foxes saw
   that their Christmas prize
Was just a wee bit oversize.

"There, my dears, now don't you worry.
I'll fix this top now in a hurry."

Benjamin Rabbit found it then
Just outside the Foxes' den.
"It seems," he thought, "most certainly,
Santa left that for my family."

"Look," he cried, "see the tree I found!"
With that he called his family round.

Then there was a merrymaking,
Rollicking, frolicking, carrot-shaking
Celebration around the tree.
All were happy as rabbits can be.

Benjamin Rabbit, with his own hand,
Sliced a carrot and made a stand.

"Now let's see how this will look
In our little chimney nook."

But right away, the children cried,
"Look, it's leaning off to one side!"

"It's too tall, that's all," said Mrs. Rabbit,
And as though it were a summer carrot,
She gave it a chop
And threw away...

the top!

Then Mistletoe Mouse just happened to see
That tiny tip of a Christmas tree.

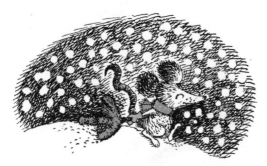

He pulled it through the snow and ice...

Up some stairs...

He fell down twice!

At last he reached his cozy house.

"It's just the right size!" said Mrs. Mouse.

Then at the top, if you please,
They put a star made out of cheese.

Oh, wasn't it grand to have a tree—
Exactly like Mr. Willowby?